MW01674758

Original title:

Soulful Connections

Copyright © 2024 Swan Charm

All rights reserved.

Author: Sara Säde

ISBN HARDBACK: 978-9916-89-016-5

ISBN PAPERBACK: 978-9916-89-017-2

ISBN EBOOK: 978-9916-89-018-9

The Echo Chamber of Us

In the silence we find our voice,
Reflecting the thoughts we all share.
Walls built high, a strange choice,
Whispers echo in the air.

Each laugh, each sigh, a mirrored sound,
Resonates deep in our core.
In this chamber, we're tightly bound,
Finding solace, yet wanting more.

We dance to rhythms of our design,
Repeating the dreams we create.
Within these bounds, our stars align,
Yet the outside world waits, sedate.

Walls reflect the light we cast,
Shadows of what could have been.
Yet in this space, we hold steadfast,
The echoes of love's sweet sheen.

But outside calls, it softly pleads,
To break the cycle, let us roam.
Beyond the echoes, new world leads,
To find a place we can call home.

The Rhythm of Our Union

In whispers soft, we find our song,
Two souls entwined, where we belong.
Each heartbeat echoes, a dance so sweet,
Together we rise, in love's heartbeat.

In laughter's glow, we share our dreams,
Through daylight's warmth and moonlit beams.
With every step, our paths align,
In unity's grace, we brightly shine.

Embers of Understanding

Beneath the stars, our stories glow,
Flickering lights in the moon's soft flow.
In silence shared, we weave our thoughts,
Embers of wisdom, love's guiding knots.

With gentle hands, we nurture sparks,
Through storms we stand, igniting arcs.
In the quiet, our minds embrace,
A fire born from trust and grace.

Resonance of Hearts

In every glance, a tale unfolds,
A symphony of whispers, our hearts behold.
Melodies bright in the dawn's sweet light,
Harmonies blending, soaring in flight.

Through trials faced, our spirits rise,
Together we chase the endless skies.
A resonance felt, with each new start,
The rhythm of life, a beat of the heart.

A Quilt of Experiences

Threads of laughter, stitches of tears,
Woven together, we've faced our fears.
Each patch a memory, vibrant and bold,
A quilt of experiences, stories retold.

In the warmth of love, we find our place,
Embracing the journey, life's sweet embrace.
Together we bind, each moment a thread,
A tapestry rich, where dreams are spread.

The Sound of Silence

In whispers soft, the shadows dwell,
Where thoughts collide, yet secrets swell.
A gentle hush, the night draws near,
The silence speaks, so loud and clear.

Amidst the void, a heartbeat sings,
A lullaby that silently clings.
The echoes fade, the stillness stays,
In quiet realms, the spirit plays.

Beneath the stars, in darkened skies,
We find our truth, where silence lies.
A tranquil space for souls to roam,
Within the quiet, we find home.

With heavy hearts, we learn to breathe,
In silence deep, we find reprieve.
The weight of words, now cast away,
In soundless nights, we truly sway.

Dreamscapes of Togetherness

In realms of dreams, where wishes flow,
Two hearts entwined, the love will grow.
Hand in hand, we chase the light,
In shared visions, all feels right.

Through drifting clouds, we find our way,
In vibrant hues, we laugh and play.
Each spark ignites the dusk's embrace,
In our dreamscape, we find grace.

A muse of hope, within our reach,
With every step, we gently teach.
Bound by warmth, we walk as one,
In dreamscapes bright, our fears are none.

With whispered thoughts, we paint the skies,
In harmony, our spirits rise.
Together strong, we face the dawn,
In dreamscapes vast, we'll carry on.

Infinite Pathways

Footsteps trace on endless ground,
In pathways lost, new hopes are found.
Through winding trails, we navigate,
Infinite choices, we contemplate.

Each turn reveals a tale to tell,
In every heartbeat, echoes swell.
A guiding star, to show the way,
In every journey, come what may.

Uncharted roads, they call our name,
Together brave, we stake our claim.
With every step, our fears subside,
In infinite pathways, we confide.

Amidst the maze, we find our truth,
In every stumble, seeds of youth.
We'll forge ahead with strength anew,
In boundless paths, just me and you.

Constellations of Affinity

In cosmic dance, our souls entwine,
A tapestry of stars that shine.
Each twinkle tells a story bright,
In constellations, we find light.

Connected hearts, across the skies,
In distant realms, our spirit flies.
With every glance, the universe sways,
In shared silences, love's embrace stays.

Through cosmic dust, our dreams unite,
In whispered hopes, we take our flight.
Galaxies bloom in perfect tune,
In constellations, we are strewn.

With every wish upon a star,
We weave our fates, no matter how far.
In patterns vast, our journey's planned,
In constellations, we stand hand in hand.

In the Silence of Togetherness

In the quiet, hearts entwine,
Breathless moments, sweet and fine.
Hands held softly, stories shared,
In this stillness, love declared.

The world outside may fade away,
In this embrace, we choose to stay.
Time suspends, a gentle tide,
In the silence, we confide.

Whispers linger in the air,
Promises made, a sacred dare.
Eyes that dance without a sound,
In this haven, peace is found.

Laughter echoes, soft and clear,
In your presence, I have no fear.
Every heartbeat, every sigh,
In the silence, I can fly.

Together, we create our space,
An uncharted, cherished place.
In this union, bright and vast,
In the silence, love holds fast.

Conversations Beyond Words

Eyes that spark with unspoken thought,
In the glance, a world is caught.
Words unneeded, feelings flow,
In your gaze, I come to know.

Minds connect like tangled vines,
Silent echoes, sweet designs.
Ideas bloom without a sound,
In this hush, truth is profound.

Time stands still, as we converse,
Every moment, a gentle verse.
Hands express what lips can't say,
In this dance, we find our way.

Heartbeats rhythm, soft and near,
In this closeness, nothing's unclear.
Like the stars that bridge the night,
In our silence, there's pure light.

Unraveled thoughts in quiet space,
In your presence, I find grace.
Conversations weave, undefined,
In the still, our souls aligned.

Dancing Shadows

Flickering lights cast playful forms,
Dancing shadows in calm storms.
With every step, a story grows,
In the twilight, magic flows.

Softly swaying, spirits rise,
In the night, the heart complies.
Whispers twirl in fleeting grace,
In this moment, time we trace.

Echoes of a distant song,
Where the shadows all belong.
Every movement, a silent call,
In this dance, we lose it all.

Lost in rhythms, side by side,
Hearts unite as dreams collide.
Underneath the moonlit veil,
In our shadows, we set sail.

Twilight's art, the evening's brush,
In this hush, we feel the rush.
Every twirl and every sway,
In the dance, we find our way.

Beneath the Surface

Ripples form in quiet streams,
Beneath the surface, life still dreams.
Hidden depths, a world unknown,
In the shadows, seeds are sown.

Gentle currents, time flows slow,
Secrets linger where few go.
In the silence, mysteries play,
Beneath the surface, lost and stray.

Echoes whisper through the dark,
Softly lighting each hidden spark.
Every wave, a secret told,
In this journey, truth unfolds.

Vistas painted, calm and deep,
In their embrace, my thoughts I keep.
Beyond the noise, serenity lies,
Beneath the surface, freedom flies.

A world of wonder, rich and vast,
In its cradle, hearts are cast.
With each pulse, a breath resounds,
Beneath the surface, love abounds.

Liminal Spaces

In shadows where the light meets day,
We wander lost, we drift away.
Between the worlds, we find our place,
In quiet moments, we embrace.

Time weaves gently, threads of dreams,
Elusive thoughts like flowing streams.
Each step deeper, we feel the pull,
Of spaces strange and beautiful.

Echoes linger in the air,
Whispers soft, a silent prayer.
Through doorways wide and paths unknown,
We search for seeds of the potent sown.

In transit, life takes on new forms,
A dance of change within the storms.
We find ourselves at every turn,
In liminal spaces, we discern.

As twilight fades to endless night,
We seek the truth beyond the light.
In every pause, in every sigh,
The liminal speaks, we learn to fly.

Tides of Togetherness

The ocean's breath pulls us near,
With every wave, we shed our fear.
United here, beneath the sky,
In salty air, our spirits fly.

Each moment shared, a drop of sea,
In endless tides, just you and me.
We dance with waves, our laughter swells,
In harmony, our story tells.

The rhythm beats, the shore does call,
As one we rise, as one we fall.
With every ebb, our hearts align,
In each embrace, we intertwine.

As sunlight fades, the stars take flight,
Our kindred souls shine in the night.
In every smile, a universe,
Together strong, we'll never curse.

In deepening bonds, we find our way,
Through storms and calm, come what may.
The tides of life will always flow,
In togetherness, our love will grow.

The Mystery of Us

In shadows cast by longing glances,
We weave the threads of sweet romances.
A puzzle framed in tender hue,
The mystery deepens, me and you.

With every laugh, a secret shared,
In quiet moments, hearts laid bare.
The spaces between, a blissful sigh,
In every question, the reasons why.

Two stories merge, a tale unique,
In hushed whispers, it's love we seek.
Through winding paths, we roam and roam,
In every heartbeat, we find home.

The stars align in whispered fate,
In the unknown, we contemplate.
With every dawn, new layers unfold,
The mystery of us, a story told.

With every tear, with every smile,
In fleeting moments, we reconcile.
Together we face what life throws,
The mystery of us forever grows.

Resonances of Respect

In every glance, a truth is found,
A sacred space where love is bound.
The whispers soft, the gestures clear,
In resonances, we hold each dear.

With open hearts, we learn to see,
The beauty in our diversity.
In dialogue, we shape and mold,
Respect as rich as tales of old.

Through winding paths, we seek to learn,
In kindness, we share, in wisdom, we yearn.
Each moment builds a bridge of grace,
In resonances, we find our place.

The echoes linger in the air,
Harmony sings, a world laid bare.
With every word, we plant a seed,
In respect's forest, we all are freed.

So let us forge a brighter way,
Where every voice can have its say.
In unity, our strength reflects,
The resonances of deep respect.

Anchored in Affection

In the harbor of your light,
My heart finds calm and grace.
Tides may rise and winds may blow,
But love will hold its place.

With whispers soft as twilight's glow,
We drift upon the sea.
Each moment shared, a precious gem,
Deep-rooted, wild, and free.

Through storms that shake our vessel strong,
We navigate the night.
Your hand in mine, the compass true,
Guides me towards the light.

In every wave, a heartbeat shared,
A song of trust we sing.
Together, through the crashing waves,
In love's embrace, we cling.

Anchored by affection's chain,
We'll weather every tide.
For in this ocean vast and wide,
Love is our steadfast guide.

Glimmers of Intimacy

In the hush of evening's glow,
Our laughter drifts like dreams.
Fingers brush, electric spark,
In the silence, it redeems.

Eyes locked in a knowing gaze,
A language soft and sweet.
Each glance ignites a secret fire,
Where every heartbeat meets.

With tender whispers, we unveil,
The corners of our soul.
It's in these glimmers, pure and bright,
That we become whole.

Moments stitched with golden threads,
In the fabric of our days.
With every secret shared and kept,
Love finds its way to blaze.

In the quiet, we explore,
The paths not yet defined.
Glimmers of our intimacy,
In the dark, they brightly shine.

Unseen Bonds

Between the spaces of our hearts,
A bond that cannot break.
Invisible yet palpable,
In every step we take.

With every laugh, a thread entwined,
With every tear, a stitch.
In shadows cast, our silhouettes,
Navigating every pitch.

Though distance may lay wide and vast,
This tether cannot fray.
For in the depths of silent nights,
Your essence lights the way.

We are tied by unseen threads,
Stronger than what's displayed.
In the whispers of the night sky,
Our connection will not fade.

In every heartbeat, echoes dance,
Defying time and place.
These unseen bonds weave through the dark,
Creating love's embrace.

Mosaic of Memories

Each moment, like a scattered tile,
Colors vivid, bright and bold.
Together, they form a masterpiece,
Of stories yet untold.

Through laughter shared and tears once shed,
The image starts to rise.
With every glance, a memory purled,
A treasure in disguise.

In silver hues of quiet nights,
And golden, sunlit days,
We piece together fragments lost,
In the woven, wild ways.

Every heartbeat paints a stroke,
Each breath, a gentle line.
A mosaic that reflects our love,
In every shape, divine.

As years unfold their tapestry,
We'll add to this grand view.
A mosaic carved from memories,
Crafted just for me and you.

Reverberations of Affection

Whispers dance in twilight's glow,
Hearts entwined in soft echo.
Moments linger, time suspended,
With each heartbeat, love ascended.

Through shadows cast in amber light,
We find solace in the night.
Every touch ignites a flame,
In the silence, call your name.

Memories woven, threads of gold,
In our arms, secrets unfold.
Glimmers of joy, soft and sweet,
In this rhythm, we are complete.

Beyond the stars, our dreams unite,
Every glance a spark, pure delight.
As the world fades into gray,
Our affection will find a way.

In the echoes, love will grow,
Guiding paths, our hearts will know.
Together we rise, forever strong,
In reverberations, we belong.

Traces of the Past

Footsteps linger on these roads,
Memories worn like heavy loads.
Echoes whisper tales of old,
In the silence, secrets unfold.

Photographs fade with time's embrace,
Yet in our hearts, they hold a place.
Laughter dances on the breeze,
The past remains, a timeless tease.

Old letters yellowed with age,
Pages turn, a treasured stage.
In each word, a breath of life,
Rekindling love in quiet strife.

As we wander through this maze,
Tracing shadows of our days.
With every step, we reminisce,
Finding beauty in what we miss.

In these traces, joy and pain,
Lessons learned, wisdom gained.
The past an echo, soft and vast,
In our souls, forever cast.

The Essence of Us

In the quiet, hearts collide,
Moments shared, no need to hide.
Every glance, a spark ignites,
In your arms, the world feels right.

Fragments woven, purest thread,
In our laughter, words unsaid.
Trust unspoken, souls align,
Together we write the divine.

Through the storms, through the calm,
In the chaos, find our balm.
Every heartbeat tells our tale,
In unity, we shall prevail.

The essence glows in twilight's hue,
In simple things, I find you.
Like a river, ever flow,
In the depths, our love will grow.

With each dawn, a gift anew,
In every whisper, love shines through.
In the essence of us, we find,
A journey shared, forever entwined.

Fragments of Infinity

Stars above, a canvas bright,
In each shimmer, dreams take flight.
Moments capture, fleeting grace,
In fragments, we find our place.

Time slips softly through our hands,
In between, a world expands.
Infinite echoes, whispers true,
In the silence, I find you.

Every heartbeat, a rhythm grand,
In the cosmos, we take a stand.
Unified in the vast unknown,
Fragments of infinity, our own.

Through the void, our spirits dance,
In the chaos, a fleeting chance.
With each breath, we paint the night,
In our union, purest light.

Fragments gather, paths align,
In the tapestry so divine.
In this journey, love's decree,
We become the infinity.

The Unfolding of Trust

In shadows cast, it starts to grow,
A quiet promise, soft and slow.
Through whispered vows, hearts intertwine,
In faith we stand, your hand in mine.

Each step we take, with care we tread,
The path ahead, our hearts we wed.
With every tear, with every laugh,
In trust, we find a sacred path.

The storms may come, the winds may sway,
But in each storm, we choose to stay.
With every dawn, we rise anew,
United strong, just me and you.

Layers shed, like petals fall,
With every secret, we hold all.
In every moment shared, we grow,
In trust, our love begins to flow.

Through trials faced, and fears laid bare,
Together strong, we learn to care.
A bond that deepens, pure and true,
In the unfolding, I trust in you.

Silent Echoes of Love

In whispers soft, the heart's prose flows,
Silent echoes where no one knows.
A glance, a touch, a tender sigh,
In quiet moments, love does fly.

The moonlit nights, in shadows dim,
Our feelings dance, our voices hymn.
In every pause, in every glance,
Echoes linger, a timeless dance.

Through stillness shared, our spirits blend,
In silence deep, our souls descend.
With hearts aligned in tranquil trust,
We find our strength, as lovers must.

Each fleeting hour, each breath we share,
In silent echoes, we lay bare.
Through unspoken words, our hearts align,
In this soft hush, your love is mine.

The world may fade, and noise may swell,
But in this silence, all is well.
For love's true song, in whisper flows,
A melody where silence grows.

Waves of Togetherness

Like tides that kiss the sandy shore,
Together strong, we rise and soar.
In every wave, a surge of grace,
In unity, we find our place.

Through sunlit days and stormy night,
We stand as one, a guiding light.
In every rise, in every fall,
Together bound, we face it all.

The sea of dreams, with currents bold,
In waves of trust, our story's told.
Each splash, each ripple on the way,
In togetherness, we choose to stay.

Through rolling waves, and peaceful seas,
In every moment, we find ease.
Hand in hand, beneath the sun,
In waves of love, we are as one.

Together we dance, we laugh, we cry,
With every wave, we reach for sky.
In harmony, our spirits blend,
In the sea of love, we never end.

Moments that Bind

In fleeting time, a glance, a smile,
Moments linger, though just a while.
In every heartbeat, stories bloom,
In tender gestures, love finds room.

Through laughter bright, and silent tears,
In every challenge, we conquer fears.
Each memory formed, a thread to weave,
In moments shared, we choose to believe.

The quiet hours, the joys we find,
In little things, our hearts aligned.
With every sunrise, a canvas clear,
In moments that bind, you are so dear.

Through the chaos and soothing calm,
In every sigh, your love, my balm.
These fleeting whispers, forever stay,
In moments cherished, we shall play.

So here we stand, with hands entwined,
Creating memories, our love defined.
In life's embrace, we choose to live,
In moments that bind, our hearts will give.

Eternal Riddles

Whispers in the silent night,
Tales of shadows take their flight.
Questions dance beneath the stars,
Truths entangled, caught in jars.

Time unveils the hidden seams,
Life and death, a twisted dream.
Every echo holds a clue,
Mysteries that call to you.

Within the heart a puzzle waits,
Locked behind the heavy gates.
Seek the keys to find the door,
Unlock the riddles, seek for more.

In each glance, a story told,
Through the ages, brave and bold.
Eternal questions fill the air,
Seeking answers everywhere.

At the end, what shall we find?
A tapestry, the threads entwined.
In the silence, wisdom heard,
Life’s great riddles, felt but blurred.

Heartstrings Across Time

Strings of fate connect our souls,
Through the storms, the light consoles.
A heartbeat echoes through the ages,
Love we find, on history's pages.

Whispers of the past remain,
In every joy and every pain.
Each heartbeat sings a timeless tune,
A dance beneath the watchful moon.

Moments shared, though worlds apart,
In the distance, binds the heart.
Every memory softly glows,
Across the years, the feeling flows.

As seasons change and rivers bend,
Connections stretch, but never end.
The tapestry of us is bright,
Woven with threads of purest light.

In the silence, a bond endures,
Across the timeline, love ensures.
No distance too great to defy,
Our heartstrings sing, they never die.

Webs of Understanding

In twilight's glow, we weave and spin,
Threads of thought, where ideas begin.
A tapestry both rich and rare,
Intertwined with love and care.

In every glance, a story shared,
In silence, all our hearts are bared.
Connections deep, like roots of trees,
Growing stronger in the breeze.

Questions linger in the air,
Curiosity, a bond so rare.
In the silence, answers call,
We unravel, together we fall.

Layers of thought, like petals unfold,
Each truth a treasure, each lesson bold.
Wisdom gathered in the night,
Webs of understanding, pure delight.

As we journey, hand in hand,
Through the mysteries, we will stand.
In this web of shared embrace,
Together we find our sacred space.

The Color of Connection

In every hue, the world ignites,
Colors dance through days and nights.
Each shade a story, bright and clear,
The color of connection dear.

Violet whispers of deep reflection,
Green embraces life's affection.
Golden rays and azure skies,
Paint the canvas where love lies.

Every person, a brush of fate,
Creating paths that illuminate.
With every color we engage,
We write the chapters, turn the page.

Through vibrant palettes, lessons learned,
In kindness, every heart discerned.
A spectrum wide, we share and grow,
In the colors of love, we glow.

As seasons shift and colors blend,
Our connections deepen, never end.
In every shade, an echo found,
The color of connection, profound.

Anchors of Belonging

In the quiet corners of our hearts,
We find the threads that bind us tight.
Roots can grow in distant lands,
Yet home is where the soul takes flight.

Shared laughter breezes through the air,
Whispers of love keep us afloat.
Each moment we cherish, a treasure rare,
In this safe harbor, we'll always quote.

Memories stitched in golden seams,
Hold us close through stormy weather.
With every heartbeat, we weave our dreams,
Anchored together, we are forever.

Through tides that rise and fall with ease,
We stand steadfast, never to part.
In the sanctuary of shared memories,
Belonging begins within the heart.

Together we chart a boundless sea,
Navigating stars that guide our way.
With every challenge, we dare to be,
Anchors of belonging, come what may.

The Warmth in a Gaze

In silence, eyes speak volumes clear,
A language only hearts can know.
The world fades when you're near,
In that gaze, love's light will glow.

In crowded rooms, you find my hand,
A gentle squeeze, a soft embrace.
In your eyes, the warmth I planned,
Fills my soul, a sacred space.

Moments linger like sweet perfume,
As time slows underneath our stare.
In the depths, I find my bloom,
A refuge wrapped in tender care.

With every glance, a story unfolds,
Of laughter, dreams, and whispered fears.
In this connection, love beholds,
A fortress built through all these years.

So let the world rush on outside,
For in our gaze, there's peace profound.
With you beside me, I abide,
In the warmth of love, I am found.

Guardians of Memories

With gentle hands, we hold the past,
Each moment etched, a cherished tale.
In photographs and laughter cast,
Guardians of memories never pale.

Together we wandered through time's maze,
Mapping joy with the light we chased.
In each story shared, love's flame stays,
In the fabric of life, we're interlaced.

Through storms that try to fade the light,
We gather strength, unwavering and true.
In the darkest hours, you spark the bright,
Reminding me of what we both knew.

The echoes of laughter, sweet and clear,
In the silence, they still resound.
Each memory gathered brings us near,
Guardians together, forever bound.

As chapters turn, we write anew,
With ink made strong from years gone by.
Our hearts, a canvas painted true,
In the gallery of love, we'll never say goodbye.

Echoes of Embrace

In the stillness of a summer night,
The world quiets, we find our place.
Wrapped in shadows, holding tight,
We dance to the echoes of embrace.

Your heartbeat sings a soothing tune,
A melody that calms my soul.
Under the watchful gaze of the moon,
In these moments, we are whole.

Each sigh and whisper, a gentle pull,
Drawing us closer, spirit to skin.
In the warmth of love, we feel so full,
As echoes of laughter begin to spin.

With every touch, a spark ignites,
Fires of passion set free our dreams.
In the depths of night, our hearts take flight,
On waves of whispers, love redeems.

So let the stars blanket our hearts,
As we savor the night’s sweet grace.
In each embrace, a fresh new start,
Together, forever, in love's embrace.

Harmony in Unspoken Words

In shadows cast, we find our light,
Silent whispers in the night,
Eyes that speak, no need for sound,
In every glance, love's truth is found.

The pause between, a sacred space,
A dance of hearts, a gentle grace,
Each heartbeat echoes, softly sways,
In unspoken words, our souls relays.

Moments linger, time stands still,
A quiet bond, a shared goodwill,
Through every sigh, a story told,
In harmony, our hearts unfold.

The world may roar, yet we remain,
In silence deep, joy and pain,
Together woven, a tapestry,
In the hush of love, just you and me.

Our voices blend, a soft refrain,
A melody that will sustain,
In the absence of the loud and bold,
Unspoken words, a love retold.

The Language of Togetherness

We speak in glances, soft and clear,
Language built with love, sincere,
Each touch a word, a gentle note,
In the symphony we've wrote.

The rhythm of heartbeats, side by side,
A melody where dreams abide,
Together we leap, together we fall,
In every silence, we hear the call.

The warmth of hands, a quiet strength,
In simple moments, we find length,
A world outside fades from view,
In togetherness, it's just us two.

From laughter bright to tears that flow,
Each moment shared helps us grow,
In the comfort of your embrace,
We create our own sacred space.

We dance through life, a graceful spin,
In the arms of love, we begin,
No words required, just souls aligned,
In this language, our hearts entwined.

Heartbeats in Sync

In the quiet night, our hearts align,
Pulses echo, a sacred sign,
With every beat, a truth we share,
In this rhythm, we find our prayer.

Together we breathe, time slows its race,
Two souls intertwined, embrace their space,
Synced in laughter, shared delight,
In the soft glow of starlit night.

With each heartbeat, a promise made,
In shadows and light, we are unafraid,
The song of us, a tender tune,
In perfect sync, beneath the moon.

Fingertips brush, electric and warm,
In your presence, I find my calm,
Together we chase both joy and strife,
In each heartbeat, the pulse of life.

In this dance, we move as one,
With every dawn, a new begun,
In the language of love, pure and true,
Our heartbeats sync, just me and you.

Kaleidoscope of Emotions

Life spins like colors, bright and wild,
A tapestry woven, each thread a child,
Moments burst forth, a vibrant hue,
In this kaleidoscope, I see you.

Laughter rings like chimes in the breeze,
Joy unfurls among the trees,
Each tear a jewel, every sigh,
In this emotional dance, we fly.

The shades of love, from soft to bold,
In every story, memories unfold,
Emotions twirl like leaves in flight,
Dancing through the day and night.

Passion ignites with a fiery glow,
In stillness, we find the flow,
Each heartbeat paints a canvas wide,
In the colors of love, we bide.

Together we weave, a fragile art,
A masterpiece formed from the heart,
Kaleidoscope dreams, vivid and bright,
In this world of feelings, you are my light.

Reflections of Companionship

In the quiet of the night, we share,
Whispers carried gently in the air.
Your laughter dances like a flame,
In this bond, we are never the same.

Through storms we stand, side by side,
In the shadows, our hearts reside.
Every challenge, we face as one,
Together we shine, brighter than the sun.

Memories painted in hues of gold,
Stories of friendship, forever told.
With every step, a journey we trace,
In reflections of companionship's embrace.

In silence, we find our truth,
A timeless bond, our cherished youth.
With every glance, a gentle spark,
Together we light up the dark.

In laughter and tears, we remain,
Through every joy and every pain.
In the tapestry of time, we weave,
Reflections of love, we truly believe.

Hearts Aligned

In the rhythm of the night, we meet,
Two hearts dancing to a steady beat.
In harmony, our souls combine,
In this moment, our hearts aligned.

With every breath, the world feels right,
Wrapped in warmth, we face the night.
In your eyes, a universe shines,
Every glance speaks, our hearts aligned.

Through the chaos, we find our peace,
In your presence, all worries cease.
In the whispers of the stars that twine,
We find our path, our hearts aligned.

As seasons change and days unfold,
In your embrace, I feel so bold.
Together we rise, a perfect design,
In love's embrace, our hearts aligned.

With laughter shared and tears we wipe,
In every moment, we find the type.
Of love so deep, it feels divine,
Forever now, our hearts aligned.

Flourish in Each Other's Grace

In the garden where we grow,
Together we bask in love’s warm glow.
In every petal, a story we trace,
We flourish in each other’s grace.

Through the seasons, hand in hand,
We cultivate dreams, crafting a strand.
In the silence, our hopes interlace,
In the beauty of life, we find our place.

With roots entwined beneath the ground,
In every smile, a joy profound.
In the dance of life, we leave no trace,
For we flourish in each other’s grace.

In the sunlight, we bloom so bright,
Guided by love, we find our light.
With every heartbeat, time cannot erase,
The love we share that fills the space.

As blossoms open, and colors blend,
With you, my dear, there’s no end.
In this vibrant world, we embrace,
Knowing we flourish in each other’s grace.

A Symphony of Kindness

In every gesture, a note we play,
A melody brightens up the day.
With gentle hearts, we find the way,
In a symphony of kindness, we sway.

The world sings softly, pure and clear,
With every smile, we're drawing near.
In harmony, our voices combine,
Creating moments, truly divine.

In the quiet acts, love is found,
In tender words, a joyful sound.
With each heartbeat, we intertwine,
In a dance, a symphony of kindness align.

Through the laughter and the tears we share,
In every battle, we show we care.
With open hearts, our spirits shine,
Together we create a space divine.

As life’s melody continues to play,
We will cherish every note, come what may.
In the orchestra of life, we define,
The beauty of love in each kind sign.

Celestial Conversations

In the stillness of the night,
Stars whisper secrets in delight.
The moon smiles with silvery beams,
Guiding us through cosmic dreams.

Galaxies twirl in graceful dance,
As celestial beings take their chance.
Messages float on stardust streams,
Connecting hearts with wondrous themes.

Light-years apart, yet so close,
The universe sings a gentle prose.
Constellations form a tapestry,
Of lives intertwined in mystery.

Each comet's tail a tale to tell,
Of love and loss, all woven well.
In the vastness, we find our place,
In celestial conversations, we embrace.

With every twinkle, a sweet reply,
Echoes of laughter beneath the sky.
Together we ponder the eternal night,
In celestial conversations, hearts ignite.

A Haven of Kindred Souls

In a garden where the wildflowers bloom,
Laughter dances, dispelling gloom.
Each spirit shines, a radiant light,
In this haven, everything feels right.

The bonds we share, forever strong,
In joyful harmony, we belong.
With open hearts, we weave our dreams,
In a sanctuary where love redeems.

Together we wander, hand in hand,
Through fields of hope, in this sacred land.
Kindred souls, a tapestry bright,
A haven of warmth, a shared delight.

Every moment, cherished and true,
In the laughter, the tears, the joy we brew.
Here is home, where we all find peace,
In this haven, our worries cease.

With whispers soft, and stories bold,
The warmth of friendship never grows old.
In this realm where hearts console,
We celebrate life, our kindred souls.

Origin of Understanding

In the silence where thoughts collide,
Seeds of wisdom, they coincide.
Every question, a pathway glows,
To the origin of understanding that flows.

When voices merge in gentle tones,
New perspectives break through old stones.
In compassion’s light, we start to see,
The truth that binds you, the truth that binds me.

Lessons learned from varied ways,
Enlightenment shines through both nights and days.
In shared stories, connections thrive,
In the origin of understanding, we arrive.

Empathy blooms in open hearts,
Creating bridges, swapping parts.
Through diverse journeys, we learn to feel,
In the origin of understanding, we heal.

Thus together, we journey forth,
Discovering worth in life's great girth.
In dialogue's embrace, wisdom we gain,
Finding unity in joy and pain.

Bridges of Existence

Across the chasms of endless night,
We build bridges with love and light.
Connecting souls, hand in hand,
Crafted from dreams, an infinite strand.

With every heartbeat, a step we take,
In unity's grace, we gently awake.
Each journey shared, a new perspective,
On bridges of existence, we find the collective.

The arches span both time and space,
In every face, we find a trace.
Of shared struggles, dreams that soar,
On bridges of existence, we explore.

Together we walk, through storm and sun,
In the dance of life, we are all one.
Each bridge we build strengthens the whole,
In the tapestry weaves, the fabric of soul.

So let us cross, with hearts aligned,
Leaving no soul in silence confined.
In the embrace of life, we shall persist,
Building bridges of existence, we coexist.

Beneath Shared Skies

Underneath the vast blue dome,
We wander while we dream,
With whispers in the twilight,
And stars begin to gleam.

In quiet moments, hearts align,
As whispers turn to songs,
The night's embrace, a gentle clasp,
In unity, where we belong.

We trace the lines of constellations,
With laughter as our guide,
Each dream a shooting star we catch,
With love, we shall abide.

Through the winds of time we sail,
Our spirits intertwined,
Each shadow cast, a memory,
Beneath the skies, we find.

When the dawn begins to break,
And colors paint the day,
We'll carry forth our stories,
Beneath the skies, we stay.

A Dance of Kindred Spirits

In the glow of twilight's grace,
Our souls begin to sway,
With every step, a heartbeat beats,
As night turns into day.

The rhythm moves us deeper in,
A bond we can't define,
With laughter flowing freely,
In unison we twine.

Each twirl a spark of memories,
In echoes of our past,
Together we create the scenes,
A tale meant to last.

As stars above us witness,
This dance we hold so dear,
Our spirits light the shadows cast,
As love dispels all fear.

With every clash, a spark ignites,
A flame that never dies,
In harmony, we'll always drift,
A dance beneath the skies.

Fireside Conversations

Crackling flames in quiet nights,
Bring warmth to weary hearts,
With shadows dancing on the walls,
As firelight gently starts.

We share our dreams and secrets here,
In confidence, we trust,
Each word a spark, a memory made,
In friendship, pure and just.

The world outside may fade away,
But here, the time stands still,
With laughter shared among the flames,
We find our hearts to fill.

As embers glow and stories swell,
Our voices intertwine,
Together we build bridges strong,
With every sip of wine.

When morning light begins to creep,
And fire turns to ash,
We'll carry forth these cherished nights,
Though moments fade too fast.

Bridges Built on Laughter

In the heart where joy resides,
Our laughter starts to bloom,
With stories shared and smiles exchanged,
We fill the deepest room.

Through playful jests, we find our peace,
As worries drift away,
Each chuckle builds a sturdy bridge,
To face another day.

With every giggle, every joke,
We weave a stronger tie,
A tapestry of memories,
That never shall run dry.

In moments light and fleeting,
Our spirits intertwine,
With laughter echoing through the years,
A love that will not pine.

And when the world seems heavy,
We'll gather near once more,
To build our bridges, side by side,
On laughter's cherished shore.

Echoes of Heartstrings

In the silence, whispers call,
Promises carved on the wall.
Heartbeats dance in tender light,
Echoes linger through the night.

Fading footsteps on the ground,
In each shadow, love is found.
Softly painted dreams unfold,
Tales of warmth in hues of gold.

Memories wrap like a shawl,
Embers glowing, never small.
In the depth, our hopes will rise,
Like the dawn in painted skies.

Through the storms, we stand as one,
Searching light, embracing sun.
In our hearts, a song we sing,
A melody of everything.

With each tear, a seed is sown,
In the garden we have grown.
Together now, we'll journey far,
With the echoes, be our star.

Whispers Beneath the Stars

Beneath the blanket of the night,
Soft whispers drift in silver light.
Heartfelt secrets shared in dreams,
Like flowing water, soft moonbeams.

Stardust dances in the sky,
While the world lets out a sigh.
In the quiet, souls align,
Speaking truths in words divine.

A promise held in cosmic breath,
Understanding blooms, defying death.
We find strength in shared despair,
Love’s embrace, a gentle care.

Through constellations, tales will form,
Guiding hearts through every storm.
Hand in hand, beneath the night,
Creating paths to endless light.

With every star, a wish we make,
Finding solace in our wake.
Together we will paint the sky,
With whispers soft, forever nigh.

Tides of Understanding

With each wave, a story flows,
Carried forth where the ocean knows.
Gentle currents hold our dreams,
In their midst, the laughter beams.

Waves of time, they ebb and swell,
Understanding shared, we tell.
In each rise, a bond is formed,
As hearts unite, we're gently warmed.

Upon the shore, we leave our mark,
Every lesson, a glowing spark.
In the tranquil depths, we dive,
Finding peace, we learn to thrive.

When the storms begin to rage,
We find comfort, turn the page.
Resilience flows like tides so strong,
In unity, we both belong.

Together, we will face the sea,
With open hearts, forever free.
In the dance of waves, we'll find,
A love that speaks, one of a kind.

Threads of Mutual Comfort

In the tapestry of life we weave,
Threads of comfort, we believe.
Stitched together through our pain,
In every joy, a sweet refrain.

Softly, softly, hands entwined,
In shared struggles, love defined.
Comfort found in silent gaze,
Together lost in gentle haze.

Woven tales of old and new,
In our hearts, the colors true.
Patterns form with every heart,
Crafting bonds that won't depart.

Through thick and thin, we will stand,
With every heartbeat, hand in hand.
In this quilt of memories bright,
Finding solace in the night.

With each journey, threads align,
Crafted love, a gift divine.
In our fabric, strength we find,
Threads of comfort, hearts combined.

The Gravity of Togetherness

In shadows we find the light,
Holding hands through the night,
Every whisper, every sigh,
Together, we learn to fly.

With laughter, we build our fate,
Boundless love, we cultivate,
In the silence, hearts unfold,
Together, we are bold.

Across the distance, souls align,
In the storm, we intertwine,
Roots that dig into the ground,
Together, we are found.

With every challenge that we face,
In our strength, we find grace,
Through the trials, hand in hand,
Together, we take a stand.

In the tapestry we weave,
Threads of hope we believe,
Every heartbeat echoes clear,
Together, we persevere.

Lighthouses of Understanding

In the fog, your voice guides me,
Shining bright, a constant sea,
With each wave, we learn to trust,
In your light, I find the just.

With hearts open, we embrace,
In vulnerability, we find grace,
Every story, a bridge we build,
With compassion, souls are filled.

In the tempest, we stand firm,
Navigating every term,
Through the darkness, we will steer,
Lighthouses of hope appear.

Together, we weather the storm,
In your light, I find my norm,
With every question, a chance to know,
Understanding helps us grow.

In the calm after the strife,
We find meaning in our life,
With connection, spirits soar,
Lighthouses forevermore.

A Symphony of Presence

In the quiet, a resonance,
Every heartbeat, pure essence,
Together, we create the sound,
A symphony profound.

With every glance, notes take flight,
Melodies in morning light,
Surrounding us like a song,
In presence, we belong.

Each moment a gentle refrain,
Harmony eases the pain,
In laughter, the chorus swells,
A symphony of heartbeats tells.

Through the changes, we compose,
In every challenge, love grows,
Together, we find the time,
In rhythm, we can climb.

In the echoes of our days,
Music dances in soft rays,
With every breath, we embrace,
A symphony of grace.

Via the Unknown

In the distance, paths unwind,
With every step, new dreams we find,
Whispers of what lies ahead,
Via the unknown, we are led.

With courage, we take that chance,
Embracing every circumstance,
In the mystery, we delight,
Via the unknown, we take flight.

Questions linger in the air,
Yet we venture, unaware,
With the stars to light our way,
Via the unknown, come what may.

In the twists of fate we trust,
With every leap, our hearts combust,
Together, we chase the dawn,
Via the unknown, we carry on.

In the journey, we create,
New horizons, we await,
With open hearts and steady hands,
Via the unknown, love expands.

Beneath the Surface

In shadows deep, where secrets dwell,
The water stirs, a silent swell.
Whispers dance on ripples' edge,
Unseen tales, a hidden pledge.

Each flicker holds a tale untold,
Of dreams long lost, of hearts so bold.
The depths conceal both fear and hope,
A labyrinth, a twisted rope.

As the moonlight weaves through dark,
It finds the light, igniting spark.
In the stillness, echoes play,
Beneath the surface, shadows sway.

A current pulls, a gentle tug,
In murky waters, life's warm hug.
With every wave, we learn to breathe,
In hidden realms, our souls reprieve.

To dive below, we find our truth,
Embracing sorrow, courage, youth.
For life descends, and yet ascends,
Beneath the surface, time transcends.

Dreamscapes of Friendship

In the quiet hours of dawn's first light,
We weave our dreams, taking flight.
With laughter shared, and secrets spilled,
A tapestry of joy is filled.

Through winding paths where shadows play,
We find our way, come what may.
Each moment spent is gold refined,
In echoing hearts, our souls aligned.

In every glance, a spark ignites,
A promise held in whispered nights.
Together we rise, together we fall,
In the dreamscape, we have it all.

Through storms we weather, hand in hand,
In a world of wonders, we understand.
The ties we forge, eternally bright,
Our friendship shines, a guiding light.

So let us dance on clouds afar,
Beneath the moon, beneath the stars.
These dreamscapes, woven deep and true,
In friendship's embrace, it's me and you.

The Embrace of Kindred Souls

In quiet moments, eyes will meet,
A silent bond, both warm and sweet.
In laughter shared, in tears we find,
The pulse of hearts, forever entwined.

Through winding roads and tangled paths,
We trace the lines of life's aftermath.
In whispered songs, our spirits soar,
In kindred embrace, we are much more.

With every story, every sigh,
We blend our dreams and learn to fly.
In sacred space, we breathe anew,
The warmth of you, the spark of true.

Through shadows cast and sunlight bright,
Together we wander through day and night.
In every heartbeat, love unfolds,
A treasure trove of kindred souls.

With hands held tight, we face the storm,
In unity, our hearts keep warm.
For in this life, what more to seek,
Than the embrace of those who speak?

Soft Murmurs of Tomorrow

In twilight's hush, the dreams align,
With gentle sounds, a sweet design.
Each whisper carries hope's soft call,
In murmurings of life, we rise or fall.

Through fields of gold, where daisies sway,
Tomorrow blooms in soft array.
A canvas bright, with colors vast,
In every moment, shadows cast.

With every dawn, a new refrain,
Of laughter's echo, joy, and pain.
We shape the future with our hands,
In quiet whispers, life expands.

So let us cherish every sigh,
The stories woven, you and I.
In softest tones, our dreams take flight,
Tomorrow's path shines ever bright.

With every heartbeat, time will show,
The beauty found in love's sweet glow.
In soft murmurs, we find our way,
Tomorrow waits, a brand new day.

Embracing Echoes

In shadows deep where whispers play,
Soft echoes call, guiding my way.
Each step I take, a story told,
Resonant dreams in heart unfold.

Time lingers sweet, a gentle breeze,
Moments dance like leaves on trees.
With every breath, I hear the sound,
Of all the love that's all around.

Through the silence, a voice breaks free,
Teaching kindness through harmony.
Embracing echoes of yesterday,
Transforming pain into ballet.

A symphony from world's embrace,
An endless journey, a sacred space.
The past and present, intertwined,
In the embrace of love, we find.

So let your heart, like music, flow,
In every note, let kindness grow.
Embracing echoes, strong and true,
We rise together, me and you.

The Tapestry of Us

We weave our dreams in threads of light,
Through laughter shared, we take to flight.
Each moment stitched, a vivid hue,
The tapestry grows; it's me and you.

In every knot, a story spins,
Of faith and love, where life begins.
Colors blend in perfect grace,
Every touch, a warm embrace.

Through storms and trials, we hold tight,
Guided by stars in the darkest night.
A tapestry crafted with care,
Binding our souls, a life we share.

Every piece tells who we are,
In the weave of life, we shine like stars.
Together, we face the great unknown,
In this tapestry, we have grown.

So let the colors blend and thrive,
In the tapestry, we feel alive.
With every thread, love's vibrant trust,
We are one, the tapestry of us.

Harmonies of the Heart

In the stillness, melodies rise,
Harmonies dance 'neath open skies.
Each note, a whisper, a sacred start,
Together we sing the song of the heart.

With every heartbeat, a rhythm flows,
Awakening dreams that softly grow.
Sonic waves in a sea of grace,
As we find our love's embrace.

In the echoes of laughter and tears,
Our symphony conquers all our fears.
With every chord, our spirits lift,
A song of love, the greatest gift.

Let the music guide us through,
In this harmony, I find you.
Together we'll craft a timeless art,
Creating a world from the beats of the heart.

So let us revel in this sweet refrain,
Through ups and downs, through joy and pain.
In every echo, we'll play our part,
Creating harmonies of the heart.

Unseen Ties

Beneath the surface, connections grow,
Unseen ties where feelings flow.
In quiet moments, hearts align,
A bond unbroken, pure, divine.

With every glance, a story shared,
Invisible threads that show we cared.
In laughter's glow, a silent vow,
Together we stand; together, now.

Life's tangled paths, we walk as one,
In shared dreams, our journey's begun.
With every challenge, we rise anew,
In unseen ties, our love shines through.

Though miles may stretch, our hearts remain,
Connected deeply through joy and pain.
The spirit dances, free from chains,
In the invisible love that sustains.

So let us cherish what we can't see,
The bonds that thrive in you and me.
In the quiet truths that never lie,
We find our strength in unseen ties.

Canvas of Connection

In colors bright, we intertwine,
Moments captured, yours and mine.
A brush of laughter, strokes of grace,
Building memories in this space.

Thread for thread, we weave our tale,
Through ups and downs, we will not pale.
A tapestry of love so fine,
In every hue, our hearts align.

With every shade, a story told,
In warmth and comfort, bold and gold.
Like stars above that light the night,
Together, we create the light.

On this vast canvas we will stand,
In artful silence, hand in hand.
Each brushstroke echoes, full of glee,
This masterpiece, just you and me.

With every glance, a spark ignites,
In this creation, all feels right.
A dance of colors in the sun,
In this connection, we're as one.

The Pulse of Affection

In every heartbeat, love does grow,
A rhythm shared, a gentle flow.
With whispers soft, we find our beat,
Together, weaving, tender and sweet.

With each touch, a spark ignites,
In quiet moments, warmth invites.
Like echoes from a distant shore,
Your presence, love, I long for more.

Through trials faced and joys we find,
A dance of souls, forever kind.
With every laugh, our spirits rise,
In this embrace, true love never lies.

In the silence, hear the song,
A melody that pulls us along.
With every glance, affection swells,
In this heartbeat, all love dwells.

With every sunset, blush and hue,
In our hearts, a bond so true.
Together moving, strong and free,
This pulse of love, just you and me.

Intertwined Journeys

Paths converge beneath the trees,
With every step, we drift like leaves.
Side by side, our dreams unfold,
In stories shared, together bold.

Across the miles, through storm and sun,
In every journey, two become one.
With laughter ringing, spirits soar,
In every moment, we explore.

Through valleys low and mountains high,
With hands clasped tight, we touch the sky.
In every twist, our hearts align,
A map of love in every sign.

In sunlit glades and shadowed lanes,
Through laughter's joys and gentle pains.
With every turn, we find our song,
In this great journey, we belong.

As seasons change and time goes on,
With every dawn, our love has drawn.
In paths entwined, we brave the storm,
Together always, hearts stay warm.

Navigating Shared Landscapes

In the vast expanse of time and space,
We chart our course, in love's embrace.
With every star that lights the way,
Together, we will seize the day.

Through hills and valleys, hand in hand,
In dreams awakened, we make our stand.
With every sunrise, hope renews,
In vibrant hues, we paint our views.

In whispered winds and gentle streams,
We find the spark of cherished dreams.
With every heartbeat, paths unfold,
In shared landscapes, our story told.

Through storms we weather, skies so bright,
In unity, we take our flight.
With every journey, lessons learned,
In every corner, love has burned.

Amongst the beauty, we have found,
In silent moments, love surrounds.
Through life's adventures, near or far,
Together, we are each other's star.

Nature's Embrace

In the whispering woods, shadows play,
Leaves dance softly, welcoming day.
Streams shimmer bright under sun's gaze,
Nature's warm arms, a soothing phase.

Mountains stand tall, a watchful eye,
Clouds drift gently, across the sky.
Flowers bloom, colors bold and grand,
Life in abundance, we understand.

Breezes carry secrets, sweet and light,
Echoing laughter in the fading night.
Creatures roam free, in harmony found,
Nature's embrace, our hearts unbound.

Each season whispers tales of old,
Stories of warmth, of courage untold.
As stars emerge in a deepening blue,
We find our peace, in nature's view.

So let us wander with open hearts,
In the beauty of nature, where love starts.
For in every leaf, and in every stream,
Lies the essence of a perfect dream.

Timeworn Bonds

In shadows cast by memories dear,
Time lines etched, stories we hear.
Hands intertwined, through thick and thin,
In silence, our journey does begin.

With laughter echoing down the halls,
And whispers soft behind closed walls.
We learned the value of holding tight,
Through storms of life, we found our light.

Each photograph holds a moment caught,
In the tapestry of love, we sought.
Through tears and joy, we rise and fall,
The thread of connection, binding us all.

Years may pass, like sands in an hourglass,
But the essence of us, will never pass.
In every heartbeat, in every sigh,
Our timeworn bonds will never die.

So cherish the love that withstands the test,
In the arms of each other, we are truly blessed.
For in every glance, and every embrace,
Life's dance is sweeter, with kinship's grace.

Beneath the Surface

In the deep waters, secrets lie,
Dreams hidden low, beneath the sky.
Ripples form as thoughts take flight,
Beneath the surface, lies the light.

The ocean's depths, a world unknown,
Creatures twirl, in silence grown.
Currents whisper songs of old,
Tales of the brave, and stories bold.

Coral gardens, a vibrant dance,
Life thrives here, in a fleeting chance.
As tides ebb and flow, we learn to see,
The beauty beneath, sets our spirits free.

In pools of stillness, we seek our truth,
Moments reflect, the wisdom of youth.
For depths are rich with lessons dear,
Beneath the surface, we face our fear.

So dive deep within, let the waters flow,
Understand the depths, let your spirit glow.
For only by searching the shadows below,
Can we find the light, let our true selves show.

Threads of Existence

In the loom of life, threads intertwine,
Colors of joy, and shadows of time.
Each stitch a moment, woven tight,
In the fabric of being, dark and light.

Connections spark, like stars in night,
Guiding our paths, shining bright.
With every choice, we add to the weave,
Writing our journeys, in what we believe.

The tapestry shifts with laughter and tears,
Threads of our hopes, confronting our fears.
In the chaos of life, patterns emerge,
A dance of existence, a soulful surge.

And as we grow, the fabric expands,
With love as the needle in our hands.
We stitch our desires, our dreams, our plans,
Creating a story unique as our spans.

So cherish each thread, both thick and thin,
For in every weave, our lives begin.
In the grand design, both rough and refined,
Lie the threads of existence, perfectly aligned.

Time-Traveled Hearts

In the whisper of the night,
Memories spark and ignite.
Threads of past, woven tight,
Leading us back to the light.

In every tick, a story spun,
Echoes of laughter, shadows run.
Hearts intertwine, never undone,
Time-traveled paths where dreams begun.

Fleeting moments, stolen glance,
Time rewinds, sweet romance.
Captured hearts in a timeless dance,
A journey fueled by happenstance.

With every pulse, a heartbeat waits,
Bound by love that time creates.
Across the ages, no heavy fates,
Just time-traveled hearts, love elates.

Beneath the stars, fate's decree,
Two souls unite in reverie.
In the tapestry of constancy,
Time-traveled hearts forever free.

The Heart’s Mosaic

Each piece of love, a different hue,
Patchwork of hearts, old and new.
Fragmented stories, we imbue,
The heart’s mosaic, bright and true.

Shattered dreams in radiant light,
Tender shards, a beautiful sight.
Every memory, day and night,
Creates a canvas, pure delight.

Colors blend in harmony,
Uniting hearts in reverie.
Through the cracks, we often see,
The strength of love, our legacy.

In laughter shared and sorrow's call,
We build a bridge, we rise, we fall.
Each piece, a tale, we heed the thrall,
The heart’s mosaic, embracing all.

Through time it grows, forever bold,
A testament of love retold.
In every shard, a truth unfolds,
The heart’s mosaic, worth more than gold.

Embers of Belonging

In the stillness, sparks arise,
Softly glowing, no disguise.
Embers dance beneath the skies,
A warmth felt in shared replies.

Fires ignite in hearts so dear,
Whispers echo, always near.
In every laugh, in every tear,
Embers of belonging appear.

In moments shared and paths entwined,
A sanctuary we will find.
Through storms that roar and winds that bind,
Embers glow, forever kind.

From ashes rise, new tales to tell,
Bridges built where shadows fell.
In every hug, the warmth we dwell,
Embers of belonging, a magic spell.

In twilight's grasp and morning's light,
Together we face each new fight.
In our hearts, forever bright,
Embers of belonging, love's insight.

Terrain of Affection

Upon the hills, our shadows play,
In valleys green where hearts sway.
The terrain of affection leads the way,
Guided by love, come what may.

With every step, the ground feels warm,
In every storm, we find the charm.
Through rugged paths, hand in palm,
In the terrain of love, our calm.

Mountains rise, challenges soar,
Yet together, we explore.
In every nook, forevermore,
The terrain of affection we adore.

Beneath the stars, our dreams unfold,
In whispered tones, our stories told.
The landscape shifts, but love is bold,
In the terrain of affection, a stronghold.

Through time and space, our roots will grow,
In every season, love's gentle flow.
Together in joy, together in woe,
In the terrain of affection, our hearts glow.

Hearts in Harmony

In whispers soft, our souls entwine,
A melody that feels divine.
Together we dance, in sync we sway,
Creating a song that lights the way.

With every beat, our rhythms blend,
A bond so deep, it knows no end.
In laughter shared, and tears that flow,
Hearts in harmony, ever aglow.

Through trials faced, hand in hand,
We conquer storms, together we stand.
Each note we play, a story told,
In this symphony, love unfolds.

As dreams take flight on hope's embrace,
We chase the dawn, find our own place.
In silence deep, or songs so bright,
Hearts in harmony, pure delight.

In every pulse, our spirits rise,
A tapestry woven under the skies.
In unity found, we shall prevail,
Together as one, we set our sail.

A Garden of Kindred Spirits

In the garden where wildflowers grow,
Kindred spirits, with hearts aglow.
Every bloom tells a tale of grace,
In this haven, we find our place.

Beneath the sun, laughter takes flight,
In gentle breezes, souls unite.
Together we sow, together we reap,
The bonds of friendship, rooted deep.

From fragrant blooms to whispered dreams,
In every corner, love softly gleams.
Here, we gather, our hearts in tune,
Under the watch of the silvery moon.

As seasons change, we stand as one,
In this sacred space, our lives are spun.
Through rain and shine, we learn and grow,
In this garden, our spirits flow.

So let us nurture this sacred land,
With kindness sown by gentle hands.
For in each petal, our hopes align,
A garden of hearts, forever divine.

Threads of Light

In the tapestry of life we weave,
Threads of light, we dare believe.
Each color vibrant, each strand aligned,
A journey shared, intertwined.

Through shadows cast, we find our way,
Guided by stars that softly play.
In every moment, a glow ignites,
Threads of light in darkest nights.

With every heartbeat, energy flows,
In love's embrace, our spirit grows.
Together we shine, brighter than gold,
In the stories of us, magic unfolds.

As day turns to dusk, and dreams arise,
We follow the path where hope lies.
In laughter and grace, our spirits soar,
Threads of light forevermore.

So hold on tight to the bonds we cherish,
In this woven world, love won't perish.
For in every thread, our essence gleams,
We are the light in the flow of dreams.

The Alchemy of Being

In the stillness of the night, we breathe,
The alchemy of being, we perceive.
Each moment precious, gold in our hands,
Transforming existence, as life demands.

Through trials faced and lessons learned,
In every challenge, a fire's burned.
With each heartbeat, we find our way,
The alchemy of light in darkening day.

In the quiet spaces, wisdom gleams,
As we awaken from shattered dreams.
With courage forged in the fires of strife,
We dance through shadows, the magic of life.

With open hearts, we seek, we hold,
In the cauldron of life, let stories unfold.
For transformation comes when we dare,
To embrace the journey, life laid bare.

So let us rise, like phoenix from ash,
Embracing the now, the fleeting flash.
In the alchemy of being, we find our song,
In every heartbeat, we all belong.

Rivers of Reciprocity

In the quiet depths of night,
Where shadows dance with light,
We share our dreams like streams,
Flowing softly, pure and bright.

Every kindness, like a drop,
Builds a river, never stops,
Together we create the flow,
Of love that overflows.

In open hearts, we find our way,
Guided by the words we say,
Each gesture, like a gentle breeze,
Brings us closer, aims to please.

As we navigate this sacred place,
The bonds we weave embrace with grace,
In this flow, we find our strength,
Rivers curve, but love knows length.

So let us dive into the stream,
Embracing hope, igniting dream,
For in the waters of the soul,
We're nourished, and we are whole.

The Connection of Kindness

Amidst the chaos of the day,
A smile can light the way,
In simple acts, we find the spark,
That ignites the deepest arc.

With every word that touches soul,
We weave a tapestry, make whole,
A hand to hold, a heart that sees,
The beauty found in gentle pleas.

Connections forged in silent vows,
Underneath the ancient boughs,
We gather strength from every guest,
In kindness, we are truly blessed.

Let laughter ring, let spirits soar,
In sharing, we open a door,
Together, we become the light,
In the darkness, shining bright.

So plant the seeds of love and care,
In every heartbeat, everywhere,
For kindness flows in endless streams,
Creating hope and vibrant dreams.

Journeys of Intimacy

Under the stars, where whispers dwell,
Two souls embark, their stories tell,
In the embrace of shared delight,
Journeys bloom in the moonlight.

With every glance, a fragile thread,
We weave the words that go unsaid,
In quiet moments, hearts collide,
In the depths, we do not hide.

Through valleys low and mountains high,
Together we will touch the sky,
Each step we take, hand in hand,
In this sacred, unbounded land.

With trust as our compass, love our guide,
We face the waves, the shifting tide,
In vulnerability, we find our peace,
In these instants, worries cease.

So let's journey on this winding road,
In the warmth of each shared load,
For intimacy is not just a place,
It's a journey, etched in grace.

Traces of the Heart

In every laugh, a memory stays,
Invisible lines of golden rays,
Traces linger in the air,
Echoes of love, soft and rare.

Through seasons that come and go,
In the roots, our stories grow,
Each moment, a mark left behind,
In the fabric of hearts intertwined.

As whispers fade, still they remain,
Within our souls, a gentle refrain,
The laughter shared, the tears we shed,
A living book, the words unsaid.

With every glance, we recognize,
The shadows dance in our eyes,
In the tapestry of life's embrace,
We carry love's enduring grace.

So treasure every tender part,
For love's a map, a work of art,
In the traces left, we find our way,
Guided by love, day by day.

Veils of Connection

In whispers shared beneath the stars,
Two souls entwined despite the scars.
Each word a strand, a gentle tie,
In silence, depth, we learn to fly.

Threads of fate weave in the night,
Bound by dreams, we find our light.
With every gaze, a story spun,
Veils of connection, we become one.

Through laughter's echo, tears that fall,
We rise again, answering the call.
A tapestry of heart and mind,
In every touch, our lives aligned.

In moments fleeting, truth revealed,
A sacred bond that fate has sealed.
Through time and distance, we will find,
Veils of connection, hearts enshrined.

With every heartbeat, love extends,
A journey shared, where sorrow bends.
With every breath, the world expands,
Together woven, hand in hand.

Mosaics of Experience

In shards of light, we paint our days,
Each moment crafted, in unique ways.
Fragments of laughter, whispers of pain,
Mosaics of experience, joy and rain.

From colors bright to shadows deep,
Our stories linger, secrets we keep.
In every break, a tale unfolds,
History written in hues of gold.

Together we gather, pieces divine,
Through trials faced, the stars align.
Each lesson learned, a tile we place,
Mosaics of experience, time won't erase.

In unity, we find our grace,
In patterns rich, we find our space.
As seasons change, our hearts remain,
Mosaics of experience, joy and pain.

With every heartbeat, life we'll weave,
In this grand tapestry, we believe.
Together we stand, our stories blend,
Mosaics of experience, it never ends.

A Canvas of Emotions

Upon this canvas, colors flow,
Each stroke a feeling, high and low.
With reds of passion, blues of calm,
A tapestry woven, heartwarming balm.

Bold splashes of joy, gentle sighs,
In every hue, the truth lies.
From love's embrace to shadows cast,
A reflection of moments, present and past.

Brush in hand, we paint our dreams,
With laughter's echo, hope redeems.
The brushstrokes dance, the palette sings,
A canvas of emotions, infinite wings.

Splattered with chaos, serene in peace,
Each frame a story, never to cease.
Bound by the colors, forever we roam,
In this gallery of feelings, we find home.

A masterpiece formed from joy and strife,
In every texture, we find life.
With each new dawn, our hearts shall blend,
A canvas of emotions, without end.

The Language of Affinity

In quiet moments, hearts converse,
A language soft, profound, diverse.
With glances shared and smiles exchanged,
The language of affinity, unarranged.

In laughter's dance and gentle sighs,
Our souls entwine, no need for lies.
With every heartbeat, feelings rise,
In simple gestures, love replies.

Unspoken words, like music flow,
In rhythms of trust, we come to know.
With every hug, a promise made,
The language of affinity, never to fade.

Through trials faced and joys embraced,
In every moment, our truth is laced.
A connection deep, a sacred thing,
The language of affinity, hearts take wing.

In the stillness, our bond ignites,
A symphony written in endless nights.
Together we rise, together we stand,
The language of affinity, hand in hand.

The Language of Hearts

In whispers soft, we find our way,
A dance of souls, come what may.
With every glance, a story told,
In silent words, our hearts unfold.

The rhythm flows, like gentle streams,
Where love is spun from tender dreams.
In every beat, a pulse divine,
Our spirits twine, forever entwined.

Through laughter bright and shadows gray,
We share the night, we seize the day.
In every tear, a joy reborn,
In love's embrace, we are adorned.

The language spoken without sound,
In every silence, love is found.
With every sigh, a breath so sweet,
In unity, our hearts compete.

Together we rise, like stars above,
In cosmic dance, we weave our love.
With hearts in tune, we journey far,
Illuminated by love's true star.

Interwoven Destinies

Two paths converge, a twist of fate,
In shadows cast, we contemplate.
Through hidden trails, our lives align,
In every step, your hand in mine.

Like threads of gold, in patterns weave,
Our hopes and dreams, we dare believe.
In gentle hands, we shape our fate,
With every choice, we celebrate.

The tapestry of time unfolds,
In vibrant hues, our story holds.
Through storms we face, we stand as one,
In every challenge, love has won.

Intertwined in every breath,
Our spirits rise, defying death.
With every heartbeat, we will grow,
A bond unbroken, forever flow.

In destinies, we find our place,
With open hearts, we embrace grace.
In every moment, love ignites,
A shared journey, as day turns to night.

The Breath Between Us

In quiet moments, still and pure,
A breath exchanged, we feel secure.
With every sigh, the world fades away,
In tranquil whispers, night meets day.

The space we share, electric and near,
In every heartbeat, I know you're here.
Between the words, a language flows,
In sacred silence, love only grows.

A gentle pause, the twilight gleams,
In every silence, we weave our dreams.
With open hearts, we dive within,
In the quiet depth, our souls begin.

The distance melts, like morning dew,
In every breath, I come to you.
With every moment, a promise made,
In the stillness, love won't fade.

The breath between us sings a song,
In every note, we both belong.
Together we stand, hand in hand,
In twilight's glow, a love so grand.

Moonlight Reflections

Beneath the moon, we find our peace,
In silver rays, our worries cease.
With every glance, the night unfolds,
In whispers soft, our truth is told.

The stars above, our silent guides,
In cosmic dance, our hearts collide.
With every shimmer, dreams take flight,
In moonlight's glow, we feel the light.

Reflections deep, in waters clear,
We search the night, with nothing to fear.
In every wave, a fleeting kiss,
In tender moments, we find bliss.

Through twilight skies, our laughter soars,
In every shadow, love restores.
With every heartbeat, we ignite,
In moonlit paths, we chase the light.

Together we wander, hand in hand,
In the glow of night, a love so grand.
With each heartbeat, the cosmos binds,
In moonlight's embrace, our hearts aligned.

Where Love Resides

In gentle whispers, hearts align,
Where eyes meet, and stars entwine.
In quiet corners, warmth resides,
A tapestry of tender tides.

Through laughter shared and tears we shed,
In every word that's lightly said.
A sanctuary wrapped in grace,
In love's embrace, we find our place.

Seasons change, yet we remain,
With open arms through joy and pain.
In simple moments, life ignites,
Where love resides, our dreams take flight.

Beneath the moon's soft silver veils,
In whispered vows, our truth prevails.
Together, we chase the fleeting light,
In every dawn, our hearts unite.

The Pulse of Unity

In crowded streets, where voices blend,
We march together, hand in hand.
A symphony of varied tones,
In harmony, our spirit grows.

Echoes of laughter fill the air,
With open hearts, we truly care.
In shared burdens, strength we find,
Entwined as one, in heart and mind.

Through every challenge, we rise tall,
A collective heart that beats for all.
In unity, our hopes ignite,
Together we embrace the light.

With every step, our souls entwined,
A force of love, uniquely designed.
Together, we stand, firm and free,
In the pulse of unity, we'll always be.

Serendipitous Meetings

A chance encounter on a street,
Two wandering souls, fate's own treat.
In unexpected smiles, hearts collide,
A world transformed, with arms opened wide.

With every glance, a spark ignites,
In the dance of laughter, pure delight.
In fleeting moments, paths align,
Two lives converge, stars start to shine.

Through whispered dreams and secret tales,
In serendipity, the heart prevails.
From random steps, connections grow,
A journey begun, with love in tow.

In every goodbye, a promise made,
In every hello, memories laid.
For in the weave of time, we find,
Serendipitous meetings nurture the mind.

Embracing the Unfamiliar

In shadows cast by the unknown,
With courage bright, our seeds are sown.
New paths await, with dreams in hand,
In every twist, we make our stand.

With every step, a heart takes flight,
In unfamiliar, we find the light.
In diverse colors, life unfolds,
Embracing stories yet untold.

Through tangled roots, we learn to grow,
In every friendship, love will flow.
In the beauty of a different place,
We find ourselves, in every face.

So let us wander, hand in hand,
Discovering the vast expanse of land.
For in the unknown, magic lies,
Embracing the unfamiliar, we rise.

Printed in the USA
CPSIA information can be obtained
at www.ICGtesting.com
LVHW022025301024
795268LV00019B/256

9 789916 890172